This is my letter to the World

That never wrote to Me—

The simple News that Nature told—

With tender Majesty

Her Message is committed

To Hands I cannot see—

For love of Her—Sweet—countrymen—

Judge tenderly—of Me

VOICES · IN · POETRY

EMILY DICKINSON   S. L. BERRY

ILLUSTRATIONS BY   DUGALD STERMER

CREATIVE ⬙ EDUCATION

Emily Dickinson as a child with siblings, left to right: Emily, Austin, Lavinia

Perhaps no poet has ever penned as many memorable lines as Emily Dickinson (1830–86). It is shocking but true that only a handful of her poems were published in her lifetime. Fame came posthumously to this reclusive New England poet, so that her well-known line, "I'm Nobody! Who are you?" may have reflected how she truly felt about her work.

What is unique about "The Belle of Amherst" are her unorthodox broken meter and slant rhymes, that famous use of dashes, a richness of metaphor seldom found in poetry old or new, and dazzling originality. Dickinson's themes were universal—eternity, immortality, heaven, hell, and nature—and her manner direct, emotional, and ruthlessly honest.

Raised in a strict Puritanical household, young Emily's parents believed a classical education indispensable. She was never comfortable with orthodox religion—"The soul should stand ajar," she wrote, "ready to welcome the ecstatic experience." This experience she found most often not in intellectual pursuits or personal relationships but in the beauty of nature and through inner reflection.

Dickinson also sought spirituality in the poems of much-admired poets such as John Keats and Elizabeth Barrett Browning, and in the deeply personal verses she wrote, alternately brooding and joyous. Dickinson's poems speak volumes in just a few words about the emotional condition of the poet, the poem's speaker, or the reader, sometimes in meanings initially obscure. Although she never wrote a long poem, her readers may need to devote more time and attention to her brief lines than they would to a longer work of literature. Perhaps Dickinson's exaggerated use of dashes was her way of telling the reader to slow down and pay close attention.

After Emily's death, her beloved sister Lavinia was instructed to burn her letters, which are poetry in themselves. Lavinia, or "Vinnie," discovered hundreds of her sister's verses, stitched together by the poet herself and subsequently published in various versions.

Of Emily Dickinson's poetry, let Australian-born essayist Clive James have the last word: She "could enamel the inside of a raindrop."

– J. Patrick Lewis, United States Children's Poet Laureate (2011-13)

"So I conclude that space & time are things of the body & have little or nothing to do with our selves. My Country is Truth."

At first, this statement by Emily Dickinson might seem odd. After all, Dickinson was one of America's most mysterious literary figures. She did all she could to disguise the truth about her life, purposely shrouding herself in a veil of secrecy and eventually withdrawing from contact with most people outside her family.

Yet what she lacked in personal candor, she made up for in literary achievement. Within the cocoon of her room on the second floor of her family home, Dickinson created poetry with such emotional and intellectual depth, and such insight into human nature that it still rings true for readers today. Many of the nearly 1,800 poems she wrote are now ranked among the world's finest, and she is recognized as one of American literature's most significant poets.

The only authenticated photograph of Emily Dickinson, dated circa 1847

Tell all the Truth but tell it slant—

Success in Circuit lies

Too bright for our infirm Delight

The Truth's superb surprise

As Lightning to the Children eased

With explanation kind

The Truth must dazzle gradually

Or every man be blind—

CHILDHOOD

Emily Elizabeth Dickinson was born on December 10, 1830, in Amherst, Massachusetts. She was the second of three children born to Edward Dickinson and Emily Norcross Dickinson. Her brother Austin was one year older, and her sister Lavinia was two years younger.

Originally, scholars believed the Dickinson household was a joyless, restrictive one, dominated by a tyrannical father. But over time that view has been modified, and it now appears that the Dickinson children were anything but meek. Their days were filled with the usual childhood activities—playing games and pranks, splashing through mud puddles, and exploring the countryside around their home. As they grew older, they went to parties, fretted over infatuations, and complained about their household chores.

Growing up, Emily was especially close to her brother Austin, sharing with him an intellectual curiosity about the world around them and a wry sense of humor about everyone in it. They discussed poetry and philosophy, and mocked boring church sermons and their father's seriousness. "You are gone, and the wheel rolls slowly on," Emily wrote in a letter to Austin after he'd returned to boarding school at the end of a holiday vacation. "Nobody to laugh with—talk with, nobody down in the morning to make the fun for me!"

An oil painting of Emily Dickinson as a child

It troubled me as once I was—

For I was once a Child—

Concluding how an Atom—fell—

And yet the Heavens—held—

The Heavens weighed the most—by far—

Yet Blue—and solid—stood—

Without a Bolt—that I could prove—

Would Giants—understand?

Life set me larger—problems—

Some I shall keep—to solve

Till Algebra is easier—

Or simpler proved—above—

Then—too—be comprehended—

What sorer—puzzled me—

Why Heaven did not break away—

And tumble—Blue—on me—

From all the Jails the Boys and Girls

Ecstatically leap—

Beloved only Afternoon

That Prison doesn't keep

They storm the Earth and stun the Air,

A Mob of solid Bliss—

Alas—that Frowns should lie in wait

For such a Foe as this—

EDUCATION

Emily Dickinson's father regarded education as essential to his children's future. While Edward wanted them to be gracious, respectable members of society, he also wanted them to be able to think for themselves. He had inherited his high regard for education from his own father, who had helped establish both of Amherst's famous educational institutions—Amherst Academy and Amherst College.

Initially, Emily attended the town's one-room school, but by the time she was 10 years old she was a student at Amherst Academy. At a time when most schools concentrated on teaching the three Rs—reading, 'riting, and 'rithmetic—the Academy was more progressive. Its students received instruction in Greek and Latin as well as in such subjects as chemistry, anatomy, and natural philosophy. They were also allowed to attend lectures at Amherst College. It was at the Academy that Emily began to exercise her literary skills. "Her compositions were strikingly original, and in both thought and style seemed beyond her years," recalled one of her teachers.

Emily also practiced writing by composing letters. She stretched herself in many of her early efforts, obviously trying to dazzle her readers with her powerful wit and skill with words. Over time, however, she came to understand that she had to tame that power if she were to be truly skillful in her use of words. "We used to think … that words were cheap & weak," she once wrote to a friend. "Now I don't know of anything so mighty."

Amherst College, 1854

To learn the Transport by the Pain—

As Blind Men learn the sun!

To die of thirst—suspecting

That Brooks in Meadows run!

To stay the homesick—homesick feet

Upon a foreign shore—

Haunted by native lands, the while—

And blue—beloved air!

This is the Sovereign Anguish!

This—the signal woe!

These are the patient "Laureates"

Whose voices—trained—below—

Ascend in ceaseless Carol—

Inaudible, indeed,

To us—the duller scholars

Of the Mysterious Bard!

A Letter is a joy of Earth—

It is denied the Gods—

"Faith" is a fine invention

When Gentlemen can see—

But *Microscopes* are prudent

In an Emergency.

At the age of 17, Emily entered Mount Holyoke Female Seminary in South Hadley, Massachusetts, about 10 miles (16 km) from Amherst. In addition to suffering from homesickness, Emily incurred the ire of administrators when she refused to sign a public declaration of faith in Christ. She left Mount Holyoke at the end of the school year. That departure marked the end of her formal education.

Emily continued to educate herself, however. She devoured the words of Shakespeare, the poems of Elizabeth Barrett Browning, the novels of George Eliot, the stories of Nathaniel Hawthorne, and the essays of Ralph Waldo Emerson. Emily knew much of the Bible by heart. She subscribed to such literary magazines as *The Atlantic* and *Harper's*. And she once remarked that her lexicon (dictionary) was her only companion.

The more she read, the more Emily became enthralled by the power of good writing. "If I read a book [and] it makes my whole body so cold no fire ever can warm me I know *that* is poetry," she once said to a friend. "If I feel physically as if the top of my head were taken off, I know *that* is poetry. These are the only ways I know it. Is there any other way?"

Textbooks from Emily's studies at Mount Holyoke

The Brain—is wider than the Sky—

For—put them side by side—

The one the other will contain

With ease—and You—beside—

The Brain is deeper than the sea—

For—hold them—Blue to Blue—

The one the other will absorb—

As Sponges—Buckets—do—

The Brain is just the weight of God—

For—Heft them—Pound for Pound—

And they will differ—if they do—

As Syllable from Sound—

*S*ome things that fly there be—

Birds—Hours—the Bumblebee—

Of these no Elegy.

Some things that stay there be—

Grief—Hills—Eternity—

Nor this behooveth me.

There are that resting, rise.

Can I expound the skies?

How still the Riddle lies!

Susan Phelps　　　*John Graves*　　　*James Parker Kimball*　　　*Henry Vaughan Emmons*

AMONG FRIENDS

Legend has it that Emily's withdrawal from the world began when she left Mount Holyoke, but in reality she led quite a busy social life for several years after her return to Amherst. Throughout her late teens and early 20s, she attended parties, entertained visitors, and exchanged letters with female and male friends alike. As a spirited young woman in a town filled with college students and instructors, she was a popular member of Amherst society.

Of course, this busy social life only deepens the mystery surrounding Emily's later withdrawal from society. Why did she pull back from the world around her and into a world of her own? Her biographer Richard B. Sewall, author of the definitive two-volume *The Life of Emily Dickinson*, speculates that Emily's increasing desire to spend her time reading and writing mattered more to her than socializing.

That argument is strengthened by a letter written by one of Emily's male friends. Describing the young women he knew in Amherst in the late 1840s, he wrote: "Em. Dickinson is a year younger it is true but older than all in mind and heart."

Pictured are some of Emily's friends from the 1850s

dwell in Possibility—

A fairer House than Prose—

More numerous of Windows—

Superior—for Doors—

Of Chambers as the Cedars—

Impregnable of Eye—

And for an Everlasting Roof

The Gambrels of the Sky—

Of Visitors—the fairest—

For Occupation—This—

The spreading wide my narrow Hands

To gather Paradise—

The Riddle we can guess

We speedily despise—

Not anything is stale so long

As Yesterday's surprise—

MUSIC

One of Emily's earliest pleasures was music. She was reportedly a gifted pianist, composing her own pieces and skillfully improvising at the keyboard late at night. Even after she began withdrawing from contact with people outside her family, she often entertained guests by playing piano for them from behind half-closed doors.

She also studied voice—a curious pursuit, considering that her own was often described as being whispery and childlike. Perhaps that's why she quickly abandoned singing and concentrated solely on the piano. As her commitment to poetry grew stronger, however, the time Emily had to devote to music diminished.

Though she ceased any personal involvement with music, Emily maintained an interest in it throughout her life. She often referred to her writing as "singing" and once commented on "the fascinating chill that music leaves." She borrowed from church hymns many of the metrical patterns she used in her poetry. And she often wrote by candlelight at night, hunched over her cherry-wood writing table as she'd once hunched over her piano, improvising tunes in the darkness.

A march from Emily's collection of sheet music

Dying at my music!

Bubble! Bubble!

Hold me till the Octave's run!

Quick! Burst the Windows!

Ritardando!

Phials left, and the Sun!

This World is not Conclusion.

A Species stands beyond—

Invisible, as Music—

But positive, as Sound—

It beckons, and it baffles—

Philosophy—don't know—

And through a Riddle, at the last—

Sagacity, must go—

To guess it, puzzles scholars—

To gain it, Men have borne

Contempt of Generations

And Crucifixion, shown—

Faith slips—and laughs, and rallies—

Blushes, if any see—

Plucks at a twig of Evidence—

And asks a Vane, the way—

Much Gesture, from the Pulpit—

Strong Hallelujahs roll—

Narcotics cannot still the Tooth

That nibbles at the soul—

From the time Emily was 18 years old until her father's death 26 years later, the Dickinson household consisted of Emily, her parents, and her sister Lavinia (whom everyone called "Vinnie"). Her brother Austin married in 1856 and lived next door in a house called "The Evergreens."

No one in her family affected Emily more deeply than her father. A prominent attorney and businessman, Edward Dickinson was active in politics and public affairs. He helped bring the first railroad line to Amherst and later served in state and national government. Preoccupied with his work, he often ignored his daughters except to remind them of their household duties. Emily's main job was cooking, which she enjoyed. In fact, her father favored her home-baked bread over any other.

As two headstrong people living under the same roof, however, Emily and her father frequently clashed, sometimes over trivial matters. One evening her father complained that Emily had given him a dinner plate that was chipped. She promptly snatched the plate from the table, took it outdoors, and smashed it on a rock "just to remind her" not to set it in front of him again.

Still, when her father died in 1874, Emily was bereft. "His Heart was pure and terrible and

I think no other like it exists," she remarked in a letter.

Emily's relationship with her mother was very different, an odd mixture of love and disdain. On one hand, Emily derided her mother for her lack of intellectual interests. "My Mother does not care for thought," Emily wrote at the age of 31. Yet when Mrs. Dickinson became an invalid after suffering a stroke a few years later, Emily and Vinnie shared the responsibility of caring for her. When their mother died in 1882, Emily was moved to write: "We were never intimate Mother and Children while she was our Mother— but Mines in the same Ground meet by tunneling and when she became Child, the Affection came."

Like Emily, Vinnie never married. She, too, chose to live out her life in the family abode known as "The Homestead"—this despite her outgoing personality and the attention of several suitors. When young, Emily regarded Vinnie as her intellectual inferior, but as they grew older, Emily came to appreciate her sister's loyalty and protectiveness. "I would like more sisters," Emily wrote, "that the taking out of one, might not leave such stillness. Vinnie has been all, so long, I feel the oddest fright at parting with her for an hour, lest a storm arise, and I go unsheltered."

Emily's father, Edward Dickinson, and her mother, Emily Norcross Dickinson

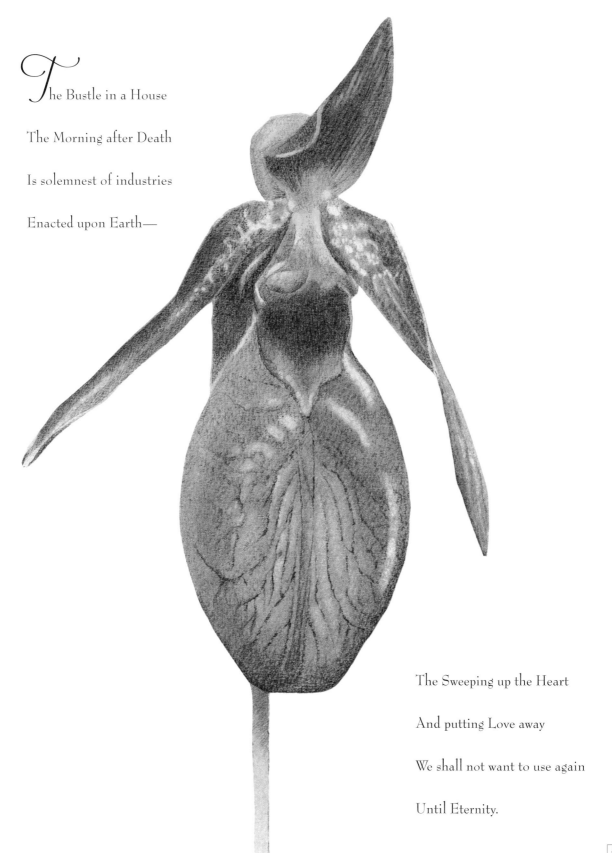

The Bustle in a House

The Morning after Death

Is solemnest of industries

Enacted upon Earth—

The Sweeping up the Heart

And putting Love away

We shall not want to use again

Until Eternity.

'Twas like a Maelstrom, with a notch,

That nearer, every Day,

Kept narrowing its boiling Wheel

Until the Agony

Toyed coolly with the final inch

Of your delirious Hem—

And you dropt, lost,

When something broke—

And let you from a Dream—

As if a Goblin with a Gauge—

Kept measuring the Hours—

Until you felt your Second

Weigh, helpless, in his Paws—

And not a Sinew—stirred—could help,

And sense was setting numb—

When God—remembered—and the Fiend

Let go, then, Overcome—

As if your Sentence stood—pronounced—

And you were frozen led

From Dungeon's luxury of Doubt

To Gibbets, and the Dead—

And when the Film had stitched your eyes,

A Creature gasped "Reprieve"!

Which Anguish was the utterest—then—

To perish, or to live?

CHRISTIANITY

One of the most crucial decisions facing Emily as a young woman was whether to join a church and declare herself a Christian. Although her father was a pious man who led his family in daily Bible readings, he didn't formally join a church until he was 47 years old. Throughout his life he was troubled by his inability to reconcile his desire to be successful in business and civic affairs with Christianity's view that earthly achievements are not as important.

Emily doubted Christianity to a greater degree than did her father. But her doubts had little to do with personal ambition and much to do with her inability to truly feel religious. "Christ is calling everyone here, all my companions have answered … and I am standing alone in rebellion," she wrote in 1850.

While many of the girls she'd grown up with in Amherst became devout Christians, Emily struggled to come to terms with her own calling. "I have perfect confidence in God & his promises & yet I know not why, I feel that the world holds a predominant place in my affections," she once noted.

Amherst First Church of Christ, attended by the Dickinsons

Some keep the Sabbath going to Church—

I keep it, staying at Home—

With a Bobolink for a Chorister—

And an Orchard, for a Dome—

Some keep the Sabbath in Surplice—

I just wear my Wings—

And instead of tolling the Bell, for Church,

Our little Sexton—sings

God preaches, a noted Clergyman—

And the sermon is never long,

So instead of getting to Heaven, at last—

I'm going, all along.

I reckon—when I count at all—

First—Poets—Then the Sun—

Then Summer—Then the Heaven of God—

And then—the List is done—

But, looking back—the First so seems

To Comprehend the Whole—

The Others look a needless Show—

So I write—Poets—All—

Their Summer—lasts a Solid Year—

They can afford a Sun

The East—would deem extravagant—

And if the Further Heaven—

Be Beautiful as they prepare

For Those who worship Them—

It is too difficult a Grace—

To justify the Dream—

WITHDRAWAL

By the time she reached her mid-30s, Emily had started to pull back from regular contact with people outside her family. While she continued to receive occasional visitors for several years, she'd begun the process of hiding away from the world that led to the mystery surrounding her today.

Since Emily's reclusiveness evolved gradually, no one in her family gave it much thought. The Dickinsons had always respected one another's individuality, and Emily's withdrawal from the world outside the family was viewed as just another one of her quirks, like her habit of playing the piano late at night. And while family friends and neighbors initially regarded Emily's behavior as odd, they, too, came to accept her reticence as a natural part of her personality.

There has been plenty of speculation about the cause of Emily's withdrawal. The most likely explanation is that it was simply part of her nature to be reclusive. Many of her close friends had married or moved out of Amherst; others were put off by Emily's refusal to become a Christian. As the world she had known as a girl changed, Emily created a new world of her own, made up of household duties, reading, letter writing, poetry, and contemplation.

The Homestead

I'm Nobody! Who are you?

Are you—Nobody—Too?

Then there's a pair of us?

Don't tell! they'd advertise—you know!

How dreary—to be—Somebody!

How public—like a Frog—

To tell one's name—the livelong June—

To an admiring Bog!

God made a little Gentian—

It tried—to be a Rose—

And failed—and all the Summer laughed—

But just before the Snows

There rose a Purple Creature—

That ravished all the Hill—

And Summer hid her Forehead—

And Mockery—was still—

The Frosts were her condition—

The Tyrian would not come

Until the North—invoke it—

Creator—Shall I—bloom?

$\mathcal{I}$ had no time to hate, because

The grave would hinder me,

And life was not so ample I

Could finish enmity.

Nor had I time to love; but since

Some industry must be,

The little toil of love, I thought,

Was large enough for me.

L O V E

Seclusion was attractive to Emily in part because it freed her from the demands of personal relationships. However, according to biographer Richard Sewall, there were three men with whom she did share herself—men with whom she was deeply in love at different points in her life. The first was Charles Wadsworth, a Presbyterian minister she met during a trip to Philadelphia in 1855. Because he was married, their relationship consisted primarily of an exchange of letters.

Emily's second love was newspaper editor Samuel Bowles. A friend of her brother's, Bowles was the first person in the publishing business she turned to when she began to seek out advice about the quality of her poetry. Though he was not very helpful or encouraging, Emily fell in love with him. Once again it was an unrequited affair, because Bowles, too, was married.

In Emily's relationship with Otis Phillips Lord, a man 18 years her senior, the love she felt was finally returned. Lord was one of the leading jurists in Massachusetts, with a seat on the Supreme Judicial Court of Massachusetts. Following his wife's death in 1877, he and Emily carried on a love affair—conducted largely by mail. However, there is evidence that they spent time together, including an indignant remark from Austin's wife about walking into the Homestead's drawing room one day and finding "Emily reclining in the arms of a man!" From Lord, Emily received her only known marriage proposal, which she turned down for reasons as mysterious as much of the rest of her life.

Still, there is no doubt that she loved Lord deeply. Following his death in 1884, Emily wrote: "I once asked him what I should do for him when he was not here, … 'Remember Me,' he said. I have kept his Commandment."

Judge Otis Phillips Lord

If you were coming in the Fall,

I'd brush the Summer by

With half a smile, and half a spurn,

As Housewives do, a Fly.

If I could see you in a year,

I'd wind the months in balls—

And put them each in separate Drawers,

For fear the numbers fuse—

If only Centuries, delayed,

I'd count them on my Hand,

Subtracting, till my fingers dropped

Into Van Dieman's Land.

If certain, when this life was out—

That yours and mine, should be

I'd toss it yonder, like a Rind,

and take Eternity—

But, now, uncertain of the length

Of this, that is between,

It goads me, like the Goblin Bee—

That will not state—its sting.

Wild Nights—Wild Nights!

Were I with thee

Wild Nights should be

Our luxury!

Futile—the Winds—

To a Heart in port—

Done with the Compass—

Done with the Chart!

Rowing in Eden—

Ah, the Sea!

Might I but moor—Tonight—

In Thee!

During the 19th century, life in America was drastically altered by the industrial revolution, the Civil War, and westward expansion. Yet, for the most part, Emily ignored these history-making events. She was devoted, instead, to the more ordinary events she observed in the natural world—seasonal changes, sunrises and sunsets, the ebb and flow of tides.

Due to the training she received at Amherst Academy, Emily had a working knowledge of biology, botany, astronomy, and geology. As a young woman, she collected ferns and wildflowers from the countryside; later in her life, she stayed close to home, puttering in the gardens that dotted the grounds around the Homestead.

Emily's interest in the natural world influenced her poetry tremendously. She referred to flowers and herbs throughout her work and used flower images as symbols. Stones and gems, stars and planets, and wildlife (especially birds) make appearances in hundreds of her poems.

Responding to a letter from her close friend, noted abolitionist and editor Thomas Wentworth Higginson, Emily wrote: "You ask of my Companions Hills—Sir—and the Sundown—and a Dog—large as myself, that my Father bought me—They are better than Beings—because they know—but do not tell."

View from Mount Holyoke, Northampton, Massachusetts, after a Thunderstorm—The Oxbow, *by Thomas Cole*

I taste a liquor never brewed—

From Tankards scooped in Pearl—

Not all the Vats upon the Rhine

Yield such an Alcohol!

Inebriate of Air—am I—

And Debauchee of Dew—

Reeling—thro endless summer days—

From inns of Molten Blue—

When "Landlords" turn the drunken Bee

Out of the Foxglove's door—

When Butterflies—renounce their "drams"—

I shall but drink the more!

Till Seraphs swing their snowy Hats—

And Saints—to windows run—

To see the little Tippler

Leaning against the—Sun—

"Nature" is what we see—

The Hill—the Afternoon—

Squirrel—Eclipse—the Bumble bee—

Nay—Nature is Heaven—

Nature is what we hear—

The Bobolink—the Sea—

Thunder—the Cricket—

Nay—Nature is Harmony—

Nature is what we know—

Yet have no art to say—

So impotent Our Wisdom is

To her Simplicity.

With the exception of six poems that appeared in newspapers at various times and another that appeared in a collection of stories and poems in 1878, Emily Dickinson never published her work. Even the poems that did show up in print were altered by editors and bore no byline.

Emily's lack of publication credits certainly wasn't because she did not try. From the 1850s on, she periodically sought the guidance of people in literary circles regarding the quality of her poetry. But she was usually rebuffed: her poems were too radical in style and structure for the conservative literary community of the time.

A collection of Emily's poems finally appeared posthumously in 1890, thanks to the efforts of her sister Vinnie and her friends Thomas Wentworth Higginson and Mabel Loomis Todd. *Poems* was an immediate sensation. Within 2 years, the book went through 11 editions. While many critics were put off by Emily's unconventional style, readers responded to her insights into human emotions.

"The face I carry with me—last," a poem written around 1862

Publication—is the Auction

Of the Mind of Man—

Poverty—be justifying

For so foul a thing

Possibly—but We—would rather

From Our Garret go

White—Unto the White Creator—

Than invest—Our Snow—

Thought belong to Him who gave it

Then—to Him Who bear

Its Corporeal illustration—Sell

The Royal Air—

In the Parcel—Be the Merchant

Of the Heavenly Grace—

But reduce no Human Spirit

To Disgrace of Price—

Much Madness is divinest Sense—

To a discerning Eye—

Much Sense—the starkest Madness—

'Tis the Majority

In this, as All, prevail—

Assent—and you are sane—

Demur—you're straightway dangerous—

And handled with a Chain—

TOWARD ETERNITY

By the time she reached her early 50s, Emily had been in seclusion for nearly 20 years. During that time, she'd ventured outside the Homestead less and less. The few outsiders who saw her often remarked on the fact that her plain white dresses were several years out of style. However, most visitors never saw Emily: if she chose to speak with them it was usually from behind a closed door or around a corner.

But her seclusion didn't make Emily immune from loss. Beginning with her father's death in 1874, she suffered the deaths of several people close to her, including her mother, her favorite nephew Gilbert (Austin's third child), and Judge Lord. When she was overcome by a nervous collapse at the age of 53, she said, "The doctor calls it 'revenge of the nerves'; but who but Death had wronged them?"

Emily recovered from that episode, but she became sick again two years later. In a letter to Thomas Wentworth Higginson, she wrote, "I have been very ill … bereft of Book and Thought." Although she was suffering from chills and lapsing into and out of consciousness, she refused to allow a doctor to examine her.

On May 13, 1886, Emily lost consciousness for the last time. Two days later, according to an entry in her brother's diary, "she ceased to breathe that terrible breathing just before the whistles sounded for six." At the age of 55, the Riddle of Amherst died.

$\mathcal{B}$ecause I could not stop for Death—

He kindly stopped for me—

The Carriage held but just Ourselves—

And Immortality.

We slowly drove—He knew no haste

And I had put away

My labor and my leisure too,

For His Civility—

We passed the School, where Children strove

At Recess—in the Ring—

We passed the Fields of Gazing Grain—

We passed the Setting Sun—

Or rather—He passed Us—

The Dews drew quivering and chill—

For only Gossamer, My Gown—

My Tippet—only Tulle—

We paused before a House that seemed

A Swelling of the Ground—

The Roof was scarcely visible—

The Cornice—in the Ground—

Since then—'tis Centuries—and yet

Feels shorter than the Day

I first surmised the Horses' Heads

Were toward Eternity—

ACKNOWLEDGMENTS

PHOTO CREDITS

Amherst College Archives; The Bettmann Archive; Corbis (Francis G. Mayer, Lebrecht Authors/Lebrecht Music & Arts), Emily Dickinson Collection in the Special Collection at the Amherst College Library; Emily Dickinson Collection, MS Am 1118.5 B74, by permission of the Houghton Library, Harvard University; Franklin Trask Library, Andover Newton Theological School; Getty Images (Mondadori Portfolio), The Granger Collection; The Jones Library, Inc., Amherst, Mass.; Mount Holyoke College Library/Archives; Nawrocki Stock Photos, Inc.; Stock Montage; Todd-Bingham Picture Collection, Yale University Library

POETRY CREDIT

From *The Complete Poems of Emily Dickinson*, edited by Martha Dickinson Bianchi. Copyright © 1924, 1935 by Martha Dickinson Bianchi; copyright © renewed 1957, 1963 by Mary L. Hampson, by permission of Little, Brown and Company. Reprinted by permission of the publishers and the Trustees of Amherst College from *The Poems of Emily Dickinson*, edited by Thomas H. Johnson (Cambridge, Mass.: Belknap Press of Harvard University Press, 1955), copyright © renewed 1955, 1979, 1983 by the President and Fellows of Harvard College.

A NOTE ON THE PUBLISHED WORKS OF EMILY DICKINSON

The first publication of Emily Dickinson's work in book form didn't take place until after her death. Published in 1890, *Poems* went through many editions before editor Thomas H. Johnson, in 1950, began the massive task of arranging the nearly 1,800 known Dickinson poems into chronological order. During that process he also established the numbering system that is now commonly used in Dickinson collections. Johnson's *The Poems of Emily Dickinson* was published by Harvard University Press in 1955 and is considered to be the definitive collection of Dickinson's works. The three-volume set has become the basis for many smaller collections as well.

INDEX

Poems appearing in this work (by first line):

Because I could not stop for Death— 44–45

The Brain—is wider than the Sky— 16

The Bustle in a House 25

Dying at my music! 22

"Faith" is a fine invention 14

From all the Jails the Boys and Girls 10

God made a little Gentian— 32

I dwell in Possibility— 19

I had no time to hate, because 33

I reckon—when I count at all— 29

I taste a liquor never brewed— 38

If you were coming in the Fall, 35

I'm Nobody! Who are you? 5, 31

It troubled me as once I was— 9

A Letter is a joy of Earth— 13

Much Madness is divinest Sense— 42

"Nature" is what we see— 39

Publication—is the Auction 41

The Riddle we can guess 20

Some keep the Sabbath going to Church— 28

Some things that fly there be— 17

Tell all the Truth but tell it slant— 7

This is my letter to the World 1

This World is not Conclusion 23

To learn the Transport by the Pain— 12

'Twas like a Maelstrom, with a notch, 26

Wild Nights—Wild Nights! 36

Amherst Academy 11, 37

Amherst College 11

Bowles, Samuel 34

Dickinson, Austin (brother) 8, 24, 34, 43

Dickinson, Edward (father) 8, 11, 24, 27, 37, 43

Dickinson, Emily Elizabeth
  childhood 5, 8,
  education 5, 11, 15
  family life 5, 6, 8, 21, 24, 30
  illness 43
  later years 43
  and music 21, 30
  and nature 37
  poetic form 5, 21, 40
  poetic themes 5, 37
  publication 5, 34, 40
  reclusiveness 5, 6, 18, 21, 30, 43
  and religion 5, 27
  romantic relationships 34
  social life 18
  on writing 11, 15, 21

Dickinson, Emily Norcross (mother) 8, 24, 43

Dickinson, Gilbert (nephew) 43

Dickinson, Lavinia (Vinnie) (sister) 5, 8, 24, 40

Higginson, Thomas Wentworth 37, 40, 43

The Homestead 24, 34, 37, 43

Lord, Otis Phillips 34, 43

Mount Holyoke Female Seminary 15, 18

Sewall, Richard B. 18, 34

Todd, Mabel Loomis 40

Wadsworth, Charles 34

Published by Creative Education

P.O. Box 227, Mankato, Minnesota 56002

Creative Education is an imprint of The Creative Company

www.thecreativecompany.us

Design by Stephanie Blumenthal

Production by The Design Lab

Illustrations by Dugald Stermer

Art direction by Rita Marshall

Printed in the United States of America

Copyright © 2015 Creative Education

Library of Congress Cataloging-in-Publication Data

Berry, S. L.

Emily Dickinson / by S. L. Berry.

p. cm. — (Voices in Poetry)

Includes index.

Summary: An exploration of the life and work of 19th-century American writer Emily Dickinson, whose poetry is known for its emotional depth as well as its unconventional rhythms and structure.

ISBN 978-1-60818-326-5

1. Dickinson, Emily, 1830–1886—Juvenile literature. 2. Women poets, American—Biography—Juvenile literature. 3. Young adult poetry, American. I. Dickinson, Emily, 1830–1886. II. Title.

PS1541.Z5B46 2014

811'.4—dc23   [B]   2013030153

CCSS: RL.4.1, 2, 3, 4, 5, 6; RL.5.2, 4, 6, 7; RI.5.1, 2, 3, 8

First Edition

9 8 7 6 5 4 3 2 1